It Takes Two *to*
TANGO

Discover How to Unlock Your Horse's Potential

TANJA MITTON

BALBOA.
PRESS
A DIVISION OF HAY HOUSE

Balboa Press books may be ordered through booksellers or by contacting:

Balboa Press
A Division of Hay House
1663 Liberty Drive
Bloomington, IN 47403
www.balboapress.com.au
1 (877) 407-4847

Print information available on the last page.

ISBN: 978-1-5043-1120-5 (sc)
ISBN: 978-1-5043-1121-2 (e)

Balboa Press rev. date: 02/09/2018

CONTENTS

FOREWORD BY
DAVID SHOOBRIDGE

As a rider, we are often busy looking for ways to develop, to improve and to consolidate work with our horses. Whether it be a pleasure rider, or an internationally competitive Grand Prix combination, we're always looking for improvement in our skill set.

Tanja Mitton's latest book reveals some wonderful systems for developing this skill set. The skill of developing harmony and clear, effective communicative messages from rider to the horse. The rider's balance, identifying the effectiveness of every aid we give, and acknowledging the control we need over our bodies and core are some of the key fundamentals behind Tanja's principles.

Riding horses from breaking-in to Grand Prix, it's evident how aware we need to be of our position and body control. Furthermore, it's imperative we understand, develop and manage a program to enhance our effectiveness, suppleness and reaction to any given action of the horse.

Traditional training scales are the most effective and proven methods of developing a horse's education. They encompass the developmental requirements of each stage of training with the view to producing a well balanced, well rounded, well educated horse. It stages the exercise, requirements and intensity of the training of the horse.

What about the rider? It is very easy to focus all our efforts on producing the best horse we can, but how can we do this without being in tune with our own requirements and functions as a rider? We need to find a system that focuses on developing our weaknesses or shortcomings into strengths and strengths into brilliance! Exercises and methods to re-balance and strengthen our core, control and build awareness of our bodies and focus and settle our minds are all aspects of professional development we can learn to adopt.

Tanja's Rider's Scale is a tool that can assist in creating priority in the way we assess our development and training. We need to be aware that, as with the traditional German Training Scale, there are processes to follow and systems in place to improve any weaknesses. Each step leads to another and is only effective if the preceding has been understood and competently executed.

Being 'rider fit' will enable our bodies to maintain our effectiveness and therefore offer the horse a regular, consistent training system that's able to be repeated time and time again. With our own control comes confidence, with confidence comes relaxation and with relaxation comes opportunity. This opportunity will be in the form of a wonderful connection, a balanced feel, or a training breakthrough. If we have this opportunity, we're more likely to be able to progress and enhance our capabilities as a rider and improve with the greatest effect.

It's vitally important that we as riders remember that horses learn through repetition. It's up to us to ensure we have a clear understanding of why, how and when we ask for a response. By following Tanja's Rider's Scale, we can ensure we have the strength, core and understanding to offer a systematic, clear plan with the ability to repeat time and time again. The end result should be a happy horse and rider combination!

This book is a wonderful reference point for riders of all stages and abilities to embrace. Read it from cover to cover and take notes, highlight, tag and copy pages. Use it as a valuable tool in self-development. It will empower the rider to take control and ownership of their riding and assist in finding a solid training foundation from which to build... and your horses will thank you for it!!

ACKNOWLEDGEMENTS

I am a great believer in teamwork and this book is an example of it.

I wouldn't have been able to put all the content together without great friends, colleagues and mentors who have provided me with ideas, feedback and help in various parts of the book.

A massive thank you goes to:

David Shoobridge for all your help and providing the foreword.

Peter and Ann-Katrin Fischer for the countless hours of brainstorming.

Angela and Michael Sausman, Lynda Page-Bickley and Sue Beattie for editing, you guys rock!

Kyrie de Jong for the drawings. 'You are an amazing artist thank you so much'.

Brooke Geary and Averil Crebbin for photos and Laura Mitton for modelling.

Lynne Harrison and Kristin Fuda for your input.

Brooke Geary for your help in putting the book together.

Fran Griffen, India Woods, Dee Vodden, Emma Schulz, Caroline Coleby, Sally Hudson for your suggestions and ideas.

And last but not least my family Richard, Laura and Jessica for your endless support, help and patience.

Introduction

*"Success is not achieved by racing to the top but rather
by building solid foundations along the way."*
- Tanja Mitton

The aim of this book is to educate riders, trainers and coaches on the fundamental principles of the rider's position and mindset. It will also explore the foundational training of horses, with the aim of developing long lasting positive outcomes for riders and horses.

The German Training Scale principles have been adopted world wide as a successful method of training horses in all disciplines, from the young novice horse all the way through to the Olympic level. The principle objective is to train horses to enhance their physical body so that the horse is able to live a long and healthy life as a riding horse.

By following the training principles correctly, going from one training level to the next and allowing horses time to develop strength and good posture, we also make sure that the horses are mentally able to cope with the training over long periods.

It is very important that all riders, trainers and coaches have a basic knowledge of the biomechanics involved for horse and rider training in order to achieve successful, longlasting outcomes.

It is here that I want to state that I don't consider myself a dressage trainer, nor am I a physiotherapist or a psychologist. My expertise is in rider posture and mindset training. However I feel compelled to share my philosophy on horse training to better explain why the riders position and mindset is so important and how they influence the horses behavior. I am a team player and therefore would always ask for input from people with more experience than myself. This book is intended to give riders more understanding on how we affect our horses and how they affect us. There are many ways of training horses and riders and I don't consider other views as right or wrong, rather different ways of achieving the same outcome.

THE SECTIONS OF THIS BOOK INCLUDE:

The newly developed *'Rider Training Scale'* is a guideline for correct riding, focusing on the rider's position and it's influence on the horse.

The modified *'Horse Training Scale'* is a training guideline on how to correctly educate a horse while keeping the rider's position in mind.

The newly developed *'Mindset Training Scale'* is a guideline for riders, coaches and trainers to help them to understand and work through their own personal issues, which will undoubtedly have a positive impact on their riding, training and coaching. A happy and confident rider/trainer/coach is better able to positively affect the training of horses and riders.

My aim for riders is to make riding easier by developing a clearer understanding of the rider's seat, as well as the horse's training scale, that can be translated and used at any level and across all disciplines. This is done by providing a step-by-step guide to achieving better outcomes from correct training.

My aim for coaches is to have a guideline that assists all coaches, with a format that they can use to teach correct rider position and develop a solid understanding of the foundations of horse training. Also to eliminate random coaching techniques and develop a more streamline approach that is used by everyone.

My aim as a mindset coach is for riders and coaches to become more aware of their own issues and develop a better understanding of how they can address and work through them to achieve their goals. This is relevant for recreational riders as well as highly competitive riders and professional trainers.

The important point I want to get across is that

Correct training = constant improvement in all areas

In my opinion not enough focus is placed on the foundations. Riders are too quick to go out and compete. A rider needs to develop their balance and correct position to correctly and effectively influence the horse. A rider who is rushed will most always become tense, lose their balance and therefore negatively influence the horse.

Horses that are rushed in their training will almost always lose relaxation and balance, which leads to tension and resistance when in a situation where the horse is under pressure. We see this very commonly at competitions where riders are nervous and horses become unbalanced and anxious.

Riders and coaches have to understand that the training scale is not a one direction, step-by-step training program. Looking at the pyramid principle, as the rider and/or horse makes progress; they must come back to the foundation levels to build greater width and stability to grow the pyramid taller. The fact that there are multiple levels within each step of the training scale might make it easier to understand the training process.

An example of this is when the horse has developed balance the next step is to improve their rhythm. As the horse becomes stronger and their rhythm improves their balance will be affected; therefore, the rider must ensure that they regularly check that the horse is still balanced within the newly developed rhythm.

As the horse becomes more supple and starts to accept the bit, the rider must ensure that the horse's rhythm remains the same and that the balance isn't compromised by the acceptance of the bit, (for example that the horse doesn't start to lean on the bit) and so on...! The foundations within the training scale can't be ticked off as they are established but rather need to be revisited and improved with every ride.

This principle also applies for the rider position training scale, the mindset training scale as well as for the horse's training scale.

The more solid the foundations are the more successful the training will be. Remember that training horses and riders is not about achieving perfection but rather to strive for constant improvement.

Let the journey begin....

The Rider's Training Scale

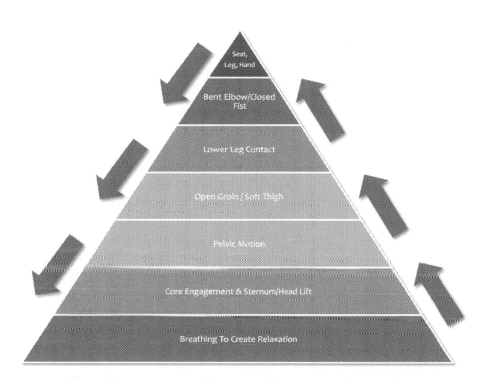

Seat,
Leg, Hand

Bent Elbow/Closed
Fist

Lower Leg Contact

Open Groin / Soft Thigh

Pelvic Motion

Core Engagement & Sternum/Head Lift

Breathing To Create Relaxation

THE RIDER'S TRAINING SCALE

"A RIDER WILL EITHER HINDER OR ENHANCE THE HORSE'S MOVEMENT,
DEPENDING ON THEIR ABILITY TO SIT CORRECTLY, LEADING TO
WORKING WITH THE HORSE INSTEAD OF AGAINST THE HORSE."
-TANJA MITTON

A rider should never underestimate the importance of their seat and the impact their position has on the horse. If the rider is lacking physical ability they will often hinder rather than help the horse. Therefore, riders should be prepared to take responsibility to improve their own personal fitness and flexibility before expecting too much from their horse. Most riders tend to focus much more on their horse's physical fitness and flexibility rather than on their own.

We all know that a horse can feel a fly landing on their body and they respond by twitching their skin. That also means that the horse feels every movement the rider makes in the saddle. When the rider is stiff, uneven or sits more to one side than the other, the horse is not only uncomfortable but also has to compensate for uneven weight distribution.

Imagine you are carrying a child on your back and the child sits crooked. How would you feel and how would your body react? What if the child does not only sit uneven but also starts moving around? How would you feel now? I think we can all relate to this example and it is easy to imagine how we would stiffen up, lose balance and brace our back to avoid injury.

It is important to understand that the more the rider expects of the horse, the fitter and more flexible the rider should be. This is where the difference lies between a recreational rider wanting to have fun and asking very little of the horse and those wanting to compete, expecting higher performance. Both the horse and the rider should be athletes to achieve cohesive performance.

Let's have a look at the rider's position and what you can do to improve your part of the team performanje.

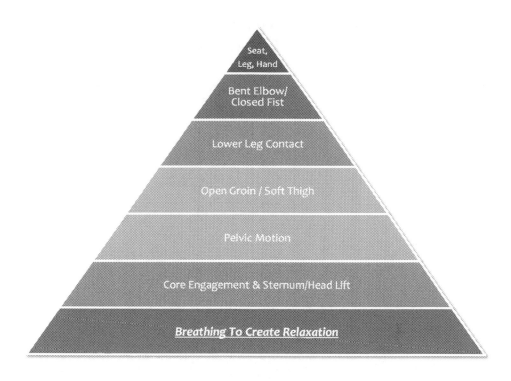

STEP 1: BREATHING TO CREATE RELAXATION

Breathing is very important, it will create relaxation. Where there is a lack of breathing, tension develops. This is because breathing is part of the autonomic nervous system and happens automatically. Most people do not really pay attention to how and when they are breathing.

Breathing has an instant effect on the body: when we breathe calmly, taking long and deep breaths out, our bodies relax. We can think more clearly and therefore make more rational decisions. When our breathing is rapid, short and shallow, we are automatically tense and tend to make more reactive decisions from a state of stress.

Many riders suffer from nerves and anxieties whether competing or just generally when riding and in both cases breathing will be compromised.

Riders who suffer from competition nerves will often be sabotaging themselves and their riding outcomes by the way they feel and what they think.

Typical thoughts are:

- *I hope I don't make a mistake.*
- *What are others thinking?*
- *What if I stuff up?*
- *I am not good enough.*
- *Everyone else is so much better than me.*
- *I don't want to let my horse down.*

Many riders at all levels and in all disciplines have thoughts such as these when it comes to competition riding. Most riders don't understand these are not simply words they are using, but that each of these words has a negative impact on their riding and ultimately the competition outcome.

BE CAREFUL WHAT YOU WISH FOR!!

There are a number of factors to consider here; firstly, the brain doesn't understand or recognize the words

- NOT
- DON'T
- WON'T

The brain only hears and focuses on the key words in a sentence. For example, when a rider thinks, 'I don't want to make a mistake' the brain only recognizes the words 'make a mistake'!

The brain doesn't recognize the difference between 'perceived' danger (I always forget the dressage test and the judge hates me!) and life threatening, 'real' danger (there is a shark in the water and he looks really hungry!); The body responds to both with an increase of adrenalin and rapid shallow breathing, producing an increase in strength and fighting power.

We are ready to take on whatever threatens our life (shark attack or judge attack).

This situation creates tension in the muscles and affects our energy, of which horses are very sensitive to and able to pick up on, no matter how small.

Horses are unable to differentiate the tension from the rider in relation to 'real danger' or 'perceived danger': a lion that is in the bush ready to pounce or the fear of what other people think of them when at a competition.

So, think twice before you think!

A horse's instinctive response to danger is to take flight.

Breathing therefore comes first on the Rider's Training Scale to allow the rider to relax their body and let go of tension; only then can the rider expect the horse to relax and work softly.

Exercises to develop the correct breathing technique:

- Take a normal, short breath in through the nose and a longer slow breath out through open lips. The rider starts to relax the mind and body when focusing on the breath out. A relaxed body is vital to develop a good position.
- Rather than breathing into the chest the rider must learn to breathe into the abdomen: breathing in, the rider's tummy

needs to expand and relax. Breathing out the rider's tummy needs to tuck in and engage. This will also lead into engaging the core.

- When breathing out the rider should have a clear intent of what they are asking the horse to do. The breath out with the intent of relaxation is used to calm the horse and lower the energy in high-energy situations, whereas the breath out with the intent of forward and more energy is used in upward transitions and an increase in energy. The intent is crucial.

- It is very important that the rider engages their core on the breath out. This automatically happens towards the end of the outward breath. Thinking about 'breathing out from your core' can be a good focus.

Breath In   Breath Out

Blowing bubbles!

A great exercise to practise correct breathing is to blow bubbles. Remember the little 'bubble blowers' kids get at birthday parties?

Imagine if you took one of these bubble blowers and tried to blow a bubble by breathing out through your nose. How do you think you would go?

Now imagine you tried to blow a bubble by blowing out a short, sharp breath. Do you think you would get good bubbles? Probably not. Now imagine you took a big breath in before breathing out, holding your bubble blower close to your mouth as you take the big breath in. How would that go??? (Sorry if you ended up with a mouth full of dish washing liquid). Now imagine you take a short breath in and a long slow breath out. How do you think you would go this time. Do you get an idea of how you need to breathe out?

Well done everyone ☺

Relaxation develops confidence and is the most important aspect of riding horses. The relaxation has to start with the rider and flow onto the horse. The rider's breath needs to feel like it sits low and deep in the body, around the belly button or even lower. This will help the rider to relax and let go of tension throughout the body as well as soften the hips. If the breath is high up in the chest area, the rider will generally tense the shoulders, the groin, the inner thigh and the hip area. This has a blocking effect on the horse, causing tension and resistance.

Too often riders and coaches blame the horse for being tense without realizing that the tension comes from the rider. Horses generally match the rider's breathing, which means that a rider who holds his breath will create a horse that holds his breath too therefore building up tension. It is also important that the rider relaxes the jaw when breathing out as many riders hold a lot of tension there. This will also assist the horse to relax their jaw and improve the acceptance of the bit (step 4 in the horse's training scale).

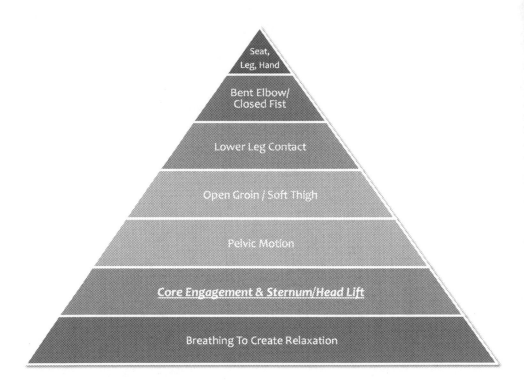

STEP 2: CORE ENGAGEMENT & STERNUM/HEAD LIFT

WHAT IS THE CORE?

The core can be thought of as a simple box with the deep abdominal muscles (Tranversus Abdominis and the Oblique muscles) making up the front, the Erector Spinae and Gluteal muscles making up the back, the pelvic floor and hip girdle muscles (Iliopsoas) making up the bottom and the diaphragm making up the roof. All of these muscles have extensive connections with the connective tissue and spine, which connects the arms and legs.

TANJA MITTON

Core muscles belong to the group of deep postural muscles that attach directly to the spine and pelvis. They are responsible for providing stability of the lumbar spine at a segmental level during movement. Lying more superficially (the outer abdominal muscles) are the large muscles (including Rectus Abdominis – 'the 6 pack' muscle) that produce movement of the trunk and provide general trunk stabilisation.

The diaphragm provides stability to the lumbar spine and core when contracted. It contracts as you breathe in and relaxes as you breathe out. Therefore, when you breathe out deeply "below your belly button", the core muscles contract and increase the pressure within the abdominal region, supporting the spine.

How does the core function?

Core stability describes the muscular control of the lower back and pelvic region to maintain functional stability; the core muscles make up a 'muscular corset' that works as a unit to stabilise the spine and torso. All movements are generated from the core and allow efficient movement of the arms and legs.

The core muscles can be engaged by gently drawing the belly button towards the spine. When the core is engaged, we should see the rider's lower back flattening out rather than being hollow which is often the case in many riders with a non-engaged core.

As the rider's lower back flattens out we can also notice that the pelvis slightly rotates; the tailbone should tuck under and the pubic bone needs to be slightly raised. This means that the rider is now sitting more on the seat bones and has less weight on the pubic bone.

Head and sternum lift

It is important that the rider looks up and straight ahead which will help the rider to maintain a head and sternum lift and a straight upper body. When the rider looks down it generally causes the sternum to drop and the rider's upper body to collapse. This is called a 'slouching' position.

Common upper body issues are:

- A rider who sits with a hollow back, which is caused by lifting the sternum too much without engaging the core first.
- A rider who leans back, again a lack of core engagement and pelvis rotation.
- A rider who slouches which is generally caused by collapsing in the sternum with or without looking down.
- Head too far forward, collapsing in the sternum and not enough sternum lift.

Hollow Back   Leaning Back   Slouching   Correct Position

The rider's upper body needs to be the same length front and back with a straight line from the rider's ears through the shoulders to the hips.

In order to develop a stable and balanced upper body the rider should be able to engage the core as well as maintaining a sternum and head lift. The rider's upper body needs to stay straight and strong yet maintain a degree of softness and suppleness to avoid tension.

Here are some great exercises:

PELVIC FLOOR

Your pelvic floor is the muscle at the bottom of your core; visualize the muscle when you do the following exercises.

- Imagine you are stopping the flow of urine and hold the contraction for 5-8 seconds and then relax.
- Next time try and hold the contraction for 5-10 seconds and then relax.

CORE EXERCISES

Planking is a great way to engage your core but make sure you engage your deep core muscles the entire time and you keep your body in a straight line from your feet to your shoulders.

- Holding a plank from your knees and elbows. This is a great way to start with a basic plank. Start out with 10-20 seconds.

- As you get more advanced hold your plank from your toes to your elbows. See if you can hold it for 20-30 seconds.

- For the very advanced you can hold the plank from your toes to your hands.

For the pros, try to work your way up to holding the plank for 60 seconds or more.

STERNUM LIFT EXERCISES

The sternum is a long flat bone in the centre of your chest, also known as the breastbone.

- To stretch your pectoral muscles, rest the left forearm flat against the doorframe at shoulder height. Step through with your left leg, taking weight onto it and rotate gently to the right. Feel the stretch through the front of your shoulder. Hold for 20 seconds and then repeat on the other side.

- Roll a large bath towel, lay it on the floor and lie on it. Make sure the towel is running lengthwise up and down your spine. Spread your arms into a T-position, palms up and let the arms hang down stretched out. Take big deep breaths and feel your ribcage expand. Hold this position for a few minutes.

HEAD LIFT EXERCISES

The head is often either too far forward or the rider is looking down at the horse's head.

- Stretch your head forwards as far as you can, then bring your head back as far as you can and then find the middle that is ideal for your head position.
- When riding, look above your horse's ears and make sure you focus ahead to where you want to go. To maintain your focus become aware of what is going on around you without getting distracted.

Head Stretched Forward   Head Stretched Back   Head in the Middle

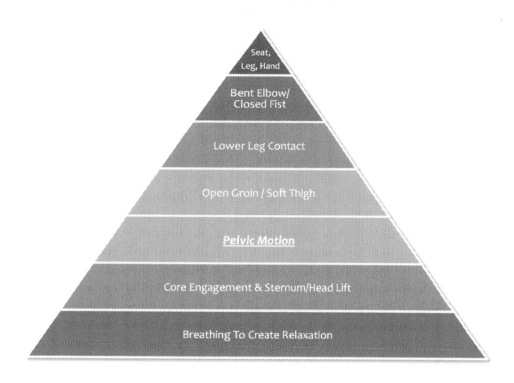

STEP 3: PELVIC MOTION

Following on from step 2 of the Rider's Training Scale, to further stabilise and balance the upper body, the rider has to learn to rotate the pelvis. By tucking the tailbone under, the rider's body is more engaged and balanced. This allows the horse to engage and balance without having to compensate for a rider who is blocking.

To engage a horse, activating their hind legs and encouraging them to lift through their back, the rider firstly must allow their hips to follow the horse's hips; the rider must activate the horse's hind leg when it is in the air and encourage it to step under. To achieve this, the rider's hips must move in harmony with the horse's hips and this can only be achieved when the rider is soft through the hips and maintains a stable, balanced body.

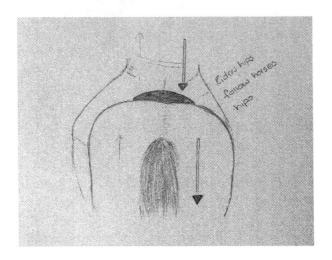

The rider's hips and horse's hips move in harmony.

For the horse's hind leg to come through and the back to stay soft the rider must make sure he/she is not blocking the horse through tightness in their own hips and inner thighs.

If the rider has a hollow back and stiff hips the horse cannot lift his back or come through from behind, but will instead develop a similar posture; a hollow back and stiff hind legs.

Horses have to compensate for the rider and this leads to horses often adopting the riders posture. This is where riders must realise that horse riding is a team sport, each team member affects the other and to achieve success both have to be an equal athlete.

SUPPLE RIDER, SUPPLE HORSE

The rider's pelvis needs to be slightly rotated so that the pubic bone lifts up. The pubic bone should have a lighter contact to the saddle than the two seat bones, which carry more of the rider's body weight. Engaging the core and tucking the tailbone under will achieve this rotation.

The rider needs to be able to stay soft in the pelvis, maintaining the rotation without hollowing the back to go with the horse. This will enable the horse to lift the back and swing as well as move the shoulders freely.

In the walk and trot the rider will feel movements of 'up and down', a 'forward and backwards' and a 'side to side'. The rider's pelvis must be able to follow these 3 movements without restricting or blocking the horse. To achieve this, the horse and rider's pelvic movements must be synchronised:

- As the horse's hind leg is in the process of stepping forward (the leg is non weight bearing) the horse's hip drops down.

- As the horse's hind leg is on the ground and in the process of stepping back (the leg is weight bearing) the horse's hip comes up.

- In the horse's forward stepping motion, the rider's hip drops, the groin relaxes and allows the thigh to openly rotate, allowing the horse's back to swing freely through without blocking. The calf comes on and encourages engagement of the hind legs. The weight of the rider's seat bone on the side stepping forward increases momentarily without tensing the seat (this movement leads to step 4 and 5 of the Rider's Training Scale).

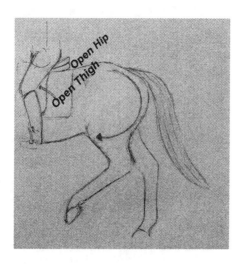

As the rider relaxes the groin and rotates the thigh out there is a 'feeling' of a slight half-moon (side to side) movement of the rider's hip as the thigh opens. This is not an actual movement of the seat bones but rather a relaxing of the inner thigh. (step 4 of the Rider's Training Scale)

In the horse's weight bearing, backward stepping motion, the rider's hip rises up and the thigh relaxes as the horse's hip also rises (this movement leads to and overlaps with step 4 of the Rider's Training Scale).

The weight of the rider's seat bone on the backward stepping side momentarily decreases as the seat bone on the forward stepping side increases. The rider's balanced seat and relaxed hips allow the rider to follow this gentle rise and fall of the horse's hips.

PELVIC MOBILITY EXERCISES

- Go on your hands and knees, drop your head, round out your mid back and round out your lower back (cat position). Hold for a few seconds. After this, go into the opposite position. Bring your head up, drop your lower back and tilt your pelvis forward (dog position). Hold this position for a few seconds too. Then go back and forth a few times always holding the new position for a few seconds.

Cat Position   Dog Position

- Start with a kneeling position where the back leg is at 90 degrees and your front leg is also at 90 degrees. Then rock your hip forward and backward.

Start

Forward Rock

- Sit on a weight bearing plastic chair and rock the chair rotating your pelvis and flattening your lower back.

Neutral Pelvis

Rotated Pelvis

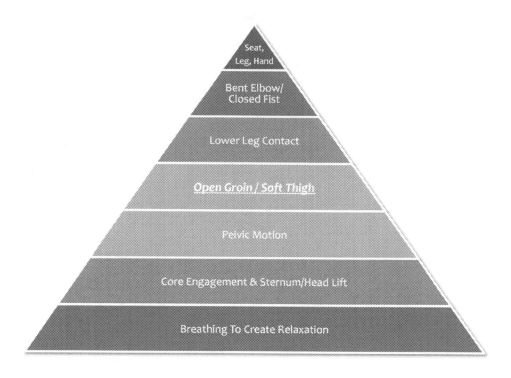

STEP 4: OPEN GROIN
AND SOFT THIGH

To open the groin the rider must learn to switch off the adductor muscle (inner thigh muscle) and strengthen the abductor muscle (outer thigh muscle) and the Piriformis muscle (lateral hip rotator muscle), as well as relax the hip flexor and gluteal muscles (this is the difference between a tight bottom and a relaxed bottom!). This allows the rider's thigh to open and sit softly on the saddle without restricting the horse's movement and bend. This position allows the rider to learn to stay soft and relaxed through the pelvis and to go with the horse's movement without interfering or blocking it (explained in step 3).

The open groin and soft thigh is also the beginning of developing the horse's acceptance of the bit as long as the rider has a soft arm that follows the rider's hip movement.

- It is important for the rider to learn to switch off the adductor muscle and switch on the abductor and Piriformis muscles. Then through continuous exercise, improve the flexibility of the groin/hip flexor to achieve the desired relaxation and open rotation which allows the movements explained in step 3 of the Rider's Training Scale.

- A relaxed open groin is vital to achieving a soft, relaxed thigh, which allows the horse to move freely forward without interference. It is important not to clench the bum cheeks when opening the groin, as this creates tension. However, tense bum cheeks are often unavoidable while the rider is strengthening the correct muscles (core, abductor and Piriformis muscles) and in turn learns to relax their hip flexors, adductor muscles and gluteal muscles.

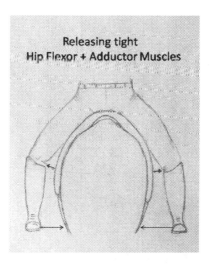

**Releasing tight
Hip Flexor + Adductor Muscles**

If the rider's adductor muscles (groin), hip flexors or Piriformis muscles are tight and tense the rider will automatically grip their thighs and restrict the horse's movements by blocking the horse's back. This makes it impossible for the horse to swing through the back and as a result the horse has to adapt his movements accordingly, this nearly always leads to the horse being hollow and tense in their back.

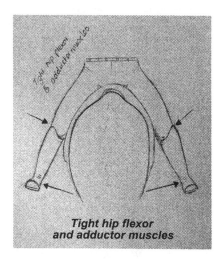

Tight hip flexor and adductor muscles

If the rider is restricted or tight in one thigh, the horse most likely learns to lean into the tight leg and tip the rider's weight to one side, which affects the horse's balance.

- Most riders are tight and restricted in their groin movement but are often unaware as it is seldom pointed out to them. This can lead to great frustration and ultimately to the rider taking shortcuts in the horse's training.

- With a stabilised and controlled upper body, a balanced pelvis and an open groin, the rider is now in a physical position to go with the horse's movement to allow the horse to swing freely. (Step 2 of the Rider's Training Scale)

For the rider to open the groin and relax the thigh they must strengthen the abductor muscles, and let go of any tension and restrictions in the hip flexors and adductor muscles, as well as relaxing the gluteal muscles. Sounds easy, doesn't it!

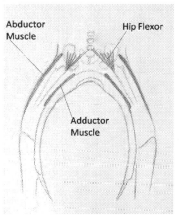
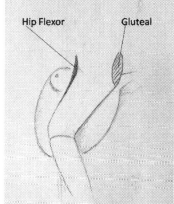

This is a process that takes time and commitment from riders to work on themselves and it can't be rushed.

Here are some great exercises for riders to improve their own groin flexibility:

- Groin resistance stretch. The rider lies on their back with their core engaged and lower back flat on the ground, the knees out to the side and heels touching each other on the ground. As the rider pushes the knees together briefly, a second person resists this and then relaxes the resistance when the rider relaxes their legs to let the knees drop down to the side. (This is known as PNF or Proprioceptive Neuromuscular Facilitation)

- The rider sits cross-legged on the floor and applies outward pressure to their knees as they also apply their own pressure by pushing up for 5 seconds. Then relax the knee pressure and push down with your arms for 5 seconds.

- Stand with your legs wide apart. Shift your weight to the left, allow your left knee to bend until it is over your left foot. You will feel the stretch in your right groin. Then repeat to the other side.

Start   Movement

- While warming up you can do a leg lift exercise. Lifting both legs off the saddle, making sure that your upper body stays straight and that you lift from your core rather than from your lower back.

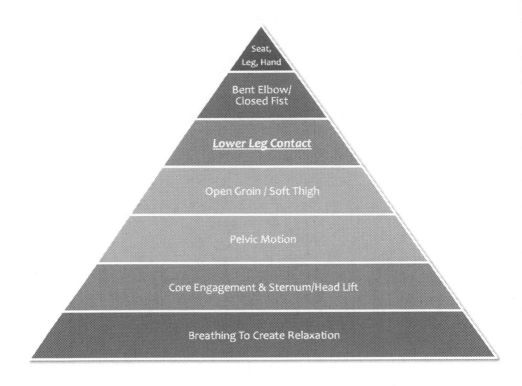

STEP 5: LOWER LEG CONTACT

With the open groin and the thigh relaxed, the rider's lower leg automatically sits on the horse better and therefore can be used more effectively. The rider must be clear with the leg aid so the horse can become confident to go forward. It is very important for the rider to learn not to block while asking the horse to go forward (blocking explained in step 4).

- With the rider's thigh open and relaxed, the 'forward' leg aid becomes clearer and horses can respond more easily.

TANJA MITTON

- When the lower leg is in an effective position, the rider's toe must be slightly turned out. If the toe is too straight the groin can't open enough and it creates tension in the ankle, which often leads to the rider rolling the ankle. If the toe is turned out too much, that also creates tension in the groin.
- The most effective part of the rider's lower leg is the back part of the inner calf. The ball of the rider's foot should be in the stirrup and evenly weight bearing to avoid the rider rolling the ankle and therefore tensing the leg.

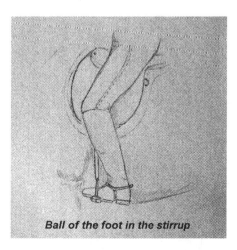

Ball of the foot in the stirrup

- The rider's toes should be evenly in line with one another and both legs in the same position to make sure the rider is sitting straight. If this is a problem, the rider may need to get his/her pelvis checked by a Chiropractor or Physiotherapist to ensure that the rider is physically able to sit straight.
- When checking the rider's lower leg position, it is important to remember that the leg is just a follow on from the pelvis and any unevenness in the leg generally can be traced back to an unevenness further up in the body (spine, hips, seat bones).
- The rider's heel needs to be the lowest point, as the leg aid comes from the calf not from the rider's heel. Spurs are to be used as a back-up of the lower leg after the leg aid and NOT instead of the leg aid.
- The strength in the lower leg increases with the relaxation of the thigh, groin, hip flexor and the engagement of the core.

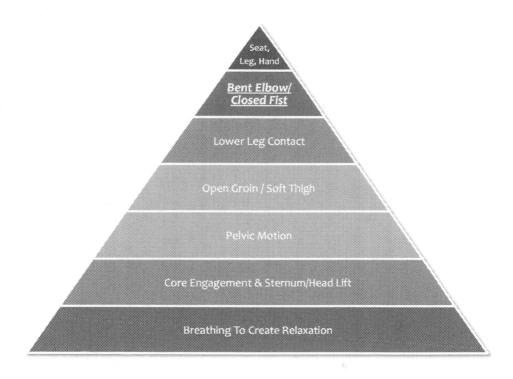

STEP 6: BENT ELBOW/CLOSED FIST

The rider's contact to the rein is very important to create and maintain softness in the horse. Softness is NOT achieved by pulling on the rein.

The rider's arm should stay soft and supple, yet consistent at all times for the horse to develop trust. A horse that is physically able and mentally relaxed will accept a contact as long as the rider is balanced and stable in their seat and able to maintain consistency and softness through a bent elbow and a closed fist (explained in the previous steps).

Bad habits

Often riders develop a bad habit of pulling on the rein, (particularly on the inside rein) and dropping the arm down in the attempt to soften the horse's poll and increase the bend.

Another bad habit that often creeps in is an open hand and a straight arm. Many riders think that an open hand is a soft hand, however what riders often don't realise is that 'no contact' leads to horses hollowing and leaning on the forehand. This in turn hinders the rider from developing balance. A loose rein also encourages a horse to become unresponsive, which then often leads to the 'horse taking over and taking the rider for a walk'.

A soft, consistent contact coming from a bent elbow and a closed fist is therefore an important part in the rider's foundation to develop an effective position.

The rider must keep the fist closed at all times to achieve a consistent contact and allow the horse to find a soft connection.

When the fist is closed the rider's arm, shoulder and elbow need to stay soft and flexible.

- To maintain a consistent contact without tension in the arm, the rider can use the thumb to apply pressure on the rein instead of tensing the fist. The rein, which is held between the little finger and the ring finger, can be held in place by applying pressure to the thumb, which is holding the rein on top of the index finger. This activates a different set of muscles and keeps the arm and elbow relaxed.

- The contact must be consistent and even, without restricting or pulling.

- The elbow stays bent to allow the arm to follow the horse's movement without restricting it.
- The thumb needs to point up and the wrist remains relaxed.

It is important that the rider has a balanced upper body first so that the rider is not relying on the reins for balance. The rider's shoulder must be relaxed and soft so that the rider's arm can go with the movements of the horse's head, this does not mean throwing away the rein.

The rider's elbow should be bent at around 120° to 130° and move in harmony with the rider's hips. This will allow the rider to develop a consistent, yet allowing, connection to the bit. Remembering that the horse's head must be allowed to move during walk and canter.

The contact to the horse's mouth must never restrict the horse from moving forward and should always allow the horse to stay open in the gullet. It is important to note that the contact does not shorten the horse's neck but allows the horse to use its neck for balance.

The fist allows the rider to maintain a steady and soft contact by being more consistent and interfere less, compared to an open hand where the contact can constantly change and interfere with the horse.

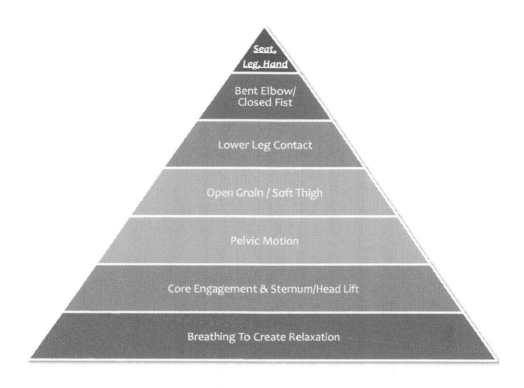

STEP 7: SEAT, LEG AND HAND CONNECTION

For the rider's seat, legs and hands to work together, the rider needs to be balanced and stable in their position. It is important to establish all the other positional points first (discussed in steps 1 to 6).

There is a German word 'Spannung' that describes the rider's complete and effective position very well. 'Spannung' means 'tautness' and this is what makes the rider's position effective without interfering with the horse's movement. If a rider's position has no 'Spannung', it is unbalanced, has no stability, no core engagement and a wobbly upper body. The horse would NOT be able to balance the rider without having to compromise their own balance.

So 'Spannung' simply means that the rider maintains stability and strength without tension and that the rider's body is independently balanced so the horse can maintain balance without having to compensate for the rider. This enables the rider's position to become effective rather than restrictive.

Seat, leg and hand connection means that the rider is able to allow the horse to move without interference and in balance, softly forward from behind and into the bit:

- The seat is well established when the rider's hips are able to go with the horse's hips, allowing the horse to swing freely and maintain softness in all gaits.
- The lower legs are used to create impulsion, riding the horse forward without restricting or blocking the horse's forwardness.
- The soft elbow and consistent contact encourages self-carriage and lightness in the horse when the horse is ready for it.

For any rider to train and educate a horse correctly they must be able to have a balanced, independent seat with a stable and controlled position.

WE NEED TO REMEMBER THAT THERE IS A DIFFERENCE BETWEEN A RIDER AND A TRAINER

An inexperienced rider is someone who is learning to go with the horse.

An experienced rider is someone who is learning to influence the horse.

A trainer is someone who can influence the horse without interfering with it.

Most riders rely on their horse for feedback on whether they are doing the right thing or not; they also rely on their horse for their confidence and how they feel about themselves as riders, which keeps them emotionally involved in the outcome of each ride and competition result.

A trainer knows from experience what 'feels' right or what 'feels' wrong. They don't need their horse to 'go well' to feel good about their own riding which allows them to stay more unemotional and objective during training.

A trainer is more likely to allow the horse to make mistakes to learn whereas a rider 'needs' the horse to go well to feel good about their riding.

The best way to improve your riding is on an older, established and educated horse where you can learn and improve your own skills. Trainers are ideally suited for younger, sensitive and green horses, where they can use their experience to increase the horse's confidence and give them a good foundation early on.

Most people who ride are 'riders' not trainers and generally underestimate how long it takes to become a trainer. Young kids or inexperienced adults are often expected to 'train' a horse without having anywhere near enough experience or feel to do so and therefore set themselves up for failure.

Think of it this way. Would we send a year ten student into a grade one class and expect them to take on the role of a teacher? No? Why not? A year ten student has all the basic skills the year one students need to learn, so why don't we do that?

Most people would argue that a year ten student hasn't got the experience to teach and that basic skill alone is not enough to make a good teacher.

And this is my point exactly. Basic riding skills do not make a trainer.

The Horse's Training Scale

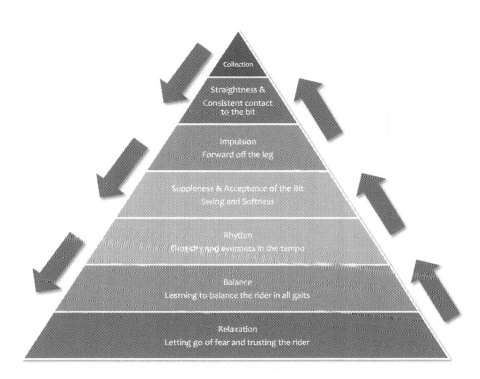

Collection

Straightness &
Consistent contact
to the bit

Impulsion
Forward off the leg

Suppleness & Acceptance of the Bit
Swing and Softness

Rhythm
Elasticity and evenness in the tempo

Balance
Learning to balance the rider in all gaits

Relaxation
Letting go of fear and trusting the rider

"TO GO FROM A RIDER TO A TRAINER TAKES ABOUT THIRTY YEARS. IT TAKES TEN YEARS TO LEARN TO GO WITH THE HORSE, THEN TEN YEARS TO LEARN HOW TO INFLUENCE THE HORSE AND ANOTHER TEN YEARS TO LEARN HOW TO INFLUENCE THE HORSE WITHOUT INTERFERING WITH IT."
- TANJA MITTON

The horse's training scale has been based on the traditional German training scale with a few slight variations that in my view have gone missing in translation. Firstly, the original training scale does not have 'relaxation' and 'balance'. I have added these two steps for the following reasons:

Relaxation and Balance are the foundation of training in any discipline. The original training scale starts with Rhythm, which in my opinion is a combination of relaxation and balance. You cannot have rhythm without the horse being relaxed first and you cannot develop rhythm without the horse having established balance. We must develop the horse's confidence. This confidence is reflected in the horses relaxation, or in the case of a lack of confidence, we see tension and anxiety.

For this reason, relaxation and balance are not regarded as part of the original German training scale but rather pre-requisites before beginning training the horse in dressage or any other discipline.

In Australia and many other countries, we have more inexperienced riders taking on the training of young horses or re-training of older horses, so it is very important to add these two components to the training scale.

Training a horse requires the rider to have a solid understanding of the horse's physical body as well as the horse's emotional state; this takes experience and skill and therefore must be taken into consideration before taking on such a horse. A young rider or an inexperienced older rider is not an ideal match for a young horse or older horse needing re-training, as neither have the experience that it takes to educate. If you are an inexperienced rider with a young horse make sure you find an experienced coach who you can work with on a regular basis to get expert help in the areas that you are not experienced in yet.

TRAINING ACCORDING TO THE TRAINING SCALE

Where many riders go wrong is that they view the training scale as a 'step by step' pyramid concept where the aim is to get to the top of the pyramid, rather than a foundation of building blocks, which need to be re-addressed regularly. Looking at the pyramid principle, it is not a race to the top but rather a sequence of steps that need revisiting and building on as the horse improves in body and strength. As the horse makes progress the rider should come back to the foundation levels to build greater width and stability, to grow the pyramid taller.

Relaxation develops confidence and trust. This is something that constantly needs to improve as the horse is exposed to different environments and more intensive training sessions.

Balance is addressing the natural crookedness of the horse by developing a more balanced posture and therefore making it easier for the horse to continue the training. Balance is a very important part of the training scale and is directly influenced by the riders seat. An unbalanced rider will never be able to develop a balanced horse.

Rhythm improves as the horse's relaxation and balance improves.

Suppleness is a result of developing abdominal muscle strength that allows the horse to lift the back, which strengthens the back muscles and makes it easier for the horse to follow the rider's seat. *Acceptance of the bit* shows that the horse has softened through the body and can follow the rider's hand. The horse has to be relaxed and balanced to achieve suppleness and accept the bit without leaning on it.

Impulsion develops with strength and the horse's ability to rotate the pelvis, engage the hind legs and activate the hocks. If the horse is not relaxed and balanced it will develop more crookedness.

Straightness improves as the horse is physically able to step straight with even weight on all four legs without adducting or abducting strides. Straightness also allows the horse to maintain a more **consistent contact**. This is when balance has fully developed.

Collection happens when the horse has developed a strong posture that allows him to carry himself and the rider easily whilst maintaining more weight in the hind legs rather then the front legs.

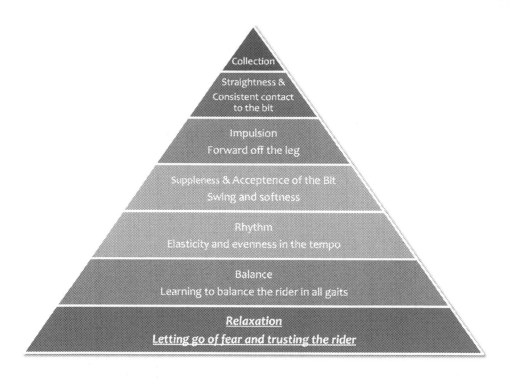

The pyramid from bottom to top:

Relaxation
Letting go of fear and trusting the rider

Balance
Learning to balance the rider in all gaits

Rhythm
Elasticity and evenness in the tempo

Suppleness & Acceptence of the Bit
Swing and softness

Impulsion
Forward off the leg

Straightness &
Consistent contact
to the bit

Collection

STEP 1: RELAXATION

BECOMING MORE CONFIDENT
AND TRUSTING THE RIDER

Relaxation is more than just the horse being quiet. It rather reflects if the horse is confident or indeed a lack of relaxation means the horse has lost its confidence.

We know that horses are flight animals and there is a fine line between relaxation and the flight instinct. When a horse feels threatened and in danger, their survival instinct takes over and they keep themselves safe by running away from danger.

Remember the first chapter of this book.

The rider's shallow breathing and tension transfers to the horse and can also trigger the horse's flight instinct.

WHAT HORSES MAY PERCEIVE AS DANGER:

- Movements in the distance they can't identify
- Negative energy they pick up in their environment
- Unfamiliar environments
- Other animals they fear as predators

THERE ARE SEVERAL WAYS THAT HORSES REACT TO FEAR:

- Horses will lift their head to 'see' where the danger is coming from. Horses can see longer distances when they raise their head up high, which then leads to a hollowing of their back; this is generally their first response when they sense 'danger' around them.

- Horses tense their back muscles, leading to a shortening and quickening of their stride.

- Shallow breathing and snorting.
- Seeking safety: this can be running/drifting back to the stable, float or other horses.
- When a horse reacts out of survival (flight response), the muscle that is connecting the jawbone to the horse's skull tightens, making it impossible for the horse to be soft in the jaw. Licking and chewing stops and the contact to the bit becomes hard and rigid. Horses tend to lean/pull on the bit and become resistant.

WHAT RIDERS PERCEIVE AS DANGER:

- The fear of falling off
- Fear of making a mistake
- Fear of being out of control
- Fear of what other people think

There are several ways that riders react to fear:

- Collapsing the sternum.
- Tensing the arms and shoulders.

- Tightening the groin and gripping with the thighs.
- Shallow breathing or 'holding their breath'.

Relaxation is therefore a priority, not only to have a 'quiet' horse, but more so to have a confident horse that can cope with their environment (competition, trail riding) and work expectation. A confident horse is a relaxed horse that has developed trust in the rider.

Relaxation creates a softening throughout the horse's body and mind and is therefore as equally important for recreational riding as it is for competition riding.

RELAXED HORSES ARE ABLE TO:

- Stay calm in the environment they work in.
- Lengthen their stride.
- Relax their poll (stretching down).
- Lick and chew on the bit (acceptance of the bit and contact).

To achieve relaxation with the horse the rider must breathe correctly and learn how to let go of their own tension, so the horse can feel safe and relaxed whilst working together (explained in the Rider's Training Scale step 1).

Horses show relaxation by breathing more deeply (ribcage is rising and falling) and taking big breaths out, (a big, soft breath out through the nostrils) this leads to the horse letting go of tension.

In much the same way as people, horses can hold a lot of tension in their jaw and for a horse to accept the bit, relaxation must come first. A horse that doesn't trust the rider will be more likely to spook and react negatively to their environment and that's why it is very important for a rider to make sure the horse trusts them wherever they are.

Exercises to establish relaxation:

BEING INSIDE A BUBBLE

Think about the 'bubble blower' concept explained in step 1 in the Rider's Training Scale. When I think of relaxation I think of the horse and rider being in a 'bubble' together. The bubble represents total focus and teamwork without distractions from the outside. Creating the 'bubble' comes from breathing correctly.

In the riders training scale, I explained that if the rider is breathing out through their nose they couldn't establish a great 'bubble'. If the rider takes a big breath in they probably end up with a mouthful of soap rather than a bubble. To blow a great bubble, the rider has to relax their jaw and breathe out softly, making the breath out long and slow.

When the horse and rider are in a 'bubble' together, the rider will feel a difference in the horse. The horse's response is generally a softening of their back and poll and a longer stride. There is a 'feeling' of relaxation. Now we know from experience that the 'bubbles' we blow don't last very long, one or two seconds at the most. The 'bubble' we create around the horse and rider is no different. Therefore, the rider must constantly blow new 'bubbles'.

To train a horse to relax we have to lead by example. Horses are so sensitive to the energy around them that they sense every bit of tension in our body and mind and this transfers to our horses.

It is therefore up to us to stay focused and 'in the bubble' to get the horse focused and 'with us' to form a successful team that can work in harmony together.

HOW DOES RELAXATION AFFECT THE HORSE'S PERFORMANCE?

True relaxation lets go of muscle tension and allows the horse to use their body to the best of their ability. This will help the horse to stay focused and soft in the environment they are being ridden and competed in, reflecting their natural movement and stage of training.

The time the horse takes to relax might vary depending on the environment and the atmosphere the horse is worked in and this is where the rider's relaxation (or lack of if the rider is nervous) greatly effects the horse. This is why relaxation has to be the first step of the Rider's and the Horse's Training Scale. The rider must understand that there are multiple levels to relaxation: relaxation has to increase as the horse is exposed to more 'scary' environments and the expectation of the horse's performance increases.

Unfortunately, too many riders make the mistake of neglecting their focus on relaxation in their training and find that horses become increasingly more tense as their expectations of the horse increases.

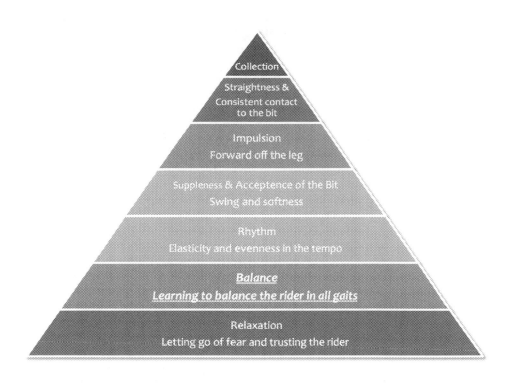

STEP 2: BALANCE

LEARNING TO BALANCE THEMSELVES AND THE RIDER IN ALL GAITS AND ACHIEVING PHYSICAL ALIGNMENT

It is very important for horses to become balanced so they learn to carry the rider evenly without putting uneven pressure on their own body that might lead to injury and soreness.

Inexperienced riders are often tempted to balance the unbalanced horse by 'holding them together with the rein' however this hinders rather than enhances the horse's balance.

Due to their curled position in utero, it is proposed that horses are born 'left' or 'right' handed, just like us. They develop their own balance by finding the easiest way to travel in their left or right 'handedness' (natural crookedness).

When a horse is started under saddle they have to adjust their balance to the rider sitting on their back, like we have to adjust our balance when we 'piggyback' another person.

Depending on how much or how little interference there is from the rider, the horse will maintain their natural left or right handedness until they have reached a stage in their training where they become even and eventually straight (ideally the rider should be independently balanced without interfering with the horse's balance - refer to position in the Rider's Training Scale).

To start the training towards straightness we first have to address the horse's horizontal and vertical balance.

HORIZONTAL AND VERTICAL BALANCE

By improving the horse's **horizontal balance** (transferring weight from the front legs into the back legs) the horse will become stronger in the back legs and find it easier to carry their rider.

This takes the pressure off the horses shoulders and front legs and also allows the horse to stay more relaxed through the neck instead of bracing the neck that comes with carrying too much weight in the front legs.

A guideline for a good horizontal balance in a young horse or an older horse during re-training is when you can draw a straight line from the horse's eye to the horse's hip while being ridden.

How to improve the horse's horizontal balance

The rider's position affects the horse's horizontal balance significantly. If the rider is tipping forward, slouching or looking down, it automatically throws extra weight onto the horse's front legs and negatively affects the horse's horizontal balance.

It is therefore very important for the rider to have good balance. The rider's stable upper body (sternum lift/core engagement), an open groin and pelvis rotation, an effective lower leg and a soft elastic arm will encourage the horse to transfer weight from the front legs to the back legs. This allows the horse to engage their abdominal muscles, rotate their pelvis under and transfer more weight onto their hind legs. Horizontal balance will improve as a result.

The rider is encouraged from time to time to lift both thighs off the saddle and release both reins to check the horse's balance. If the horse is in balance the tempo and frame should stay the same.

The rider's leg lift is exaggerated in this picture only for demonstration purposes. A much more subtle movement is generally sufficient.

Naturally a horse is heavier in the front half of their body. Depending on the horse's natural confirmation and posture this can be a little or a lot. Most horses therefore find it easier to 'pull' forward with their chest rather than 'pushing' forward from behind.

A horse that 'pulls' forward uses very little core engagement and drags their hind legs behind them. A horse that moves in this fashion will be hollow and restricted in the back and tense in the neck. These horses overdevelop the bottom of their neck due to "pulling" rather than developing the top of the neck through "pushing".

The horizontal balance needs to be addressed prior to working on the vertical balance.

Vertical balance (side to side) will allow horses to carry more even weight in all four legs rather than leaning to one side.

How to improve the horse's vertical balance

In the process of improving the horse's vertical balance, the rider needs to become aware of the horse drifting as this can indicate the horse's left or right handedness. The sooner horses develop their muscles evenly, the easier they will find straightness training later on. It is important that the rider not only feels when the horse is drifting but is able to correct the drift by using their seat correctly. An inexperienced rider will easily be shifted in their seat and end up contributing to the horse's crookedness. It takes a rider with a well established, balanced, independent seat to be able to influence the horse's balance. To establish balance in the horse the rider has to be able to stay balanced even though it will feel crooked at first. By maintaining their seat and not going with the horse's drift the rider will eventually be able to encourage the horse to take more weight into their weaker (swinging) hind leg and therefore lessen the weight on the heavier shoulder.

Because the horse is naturally crooked we have to address this issue in the horse before we can move on to the next level in the training scale.

The horse's natural crookedness

Horses, like people, tend to be left or right handed.

For example, a left-handed horse is placing more weight on the left front leg and in the left hind leg and not enough weight in the right hind leg, which is generally referred to as the 'swinging' leg. The swinging leg often doesn't step through straight but rather 'adducts' slightly inwards underneath the horses body.

A right-handed horse places more weight in the right front leg and right hind leg and not enough weight in the left hind leg (swinging leg)

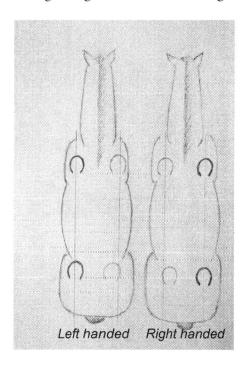

Left handed   Right handed

LET'S LOOK AT A HORSE THAT IS LEFT HANDED. THEY TEND TO HOLLOW AND OVER BEND TO THE RIGHT:

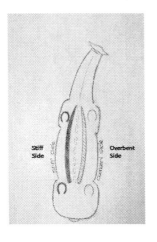

- Hollowing means that the muscle on the right side of the spine is more flexible; the muscle on the left side of the spine is stiffer.
- The horse finds it easier to contract the right side of its ribcage.
- The horse finds it easier to bend the neck to the right.
- Also, the right hind leg is the more 'swinging' leg (steps more forward) and can land slightly adducted (across), transferring the weight onto the left front leg. This is often described as the horse dropping in or falling out through the (left) shoulder.
- As a result, these horses often move on three tracks instead of two (hind leg adducting) and in some extreme cases even on four tracks.
- A left-handed horse increases the stress on the left forelimb joints and lameness is often seen in the left front leg/shoulder as a result.

Left handed horse going to the left

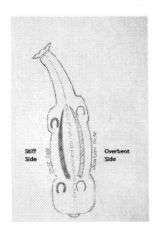

- The same left-handed horse going on the left rein would be stiffer and less able to bend to the left side due to the left back muscle and ribcage being stiffer.
- The horse finds it harder to contract and bend the left ribcage.
- The neck doesn't bend as easily to the left and some horses tend to tilt their head because of resistance in the lower part of the neck.

- The left hind leg generally steps though straighter but also steps short due to the restriction in the left shoulder.
- The horse is generally able to produce a greater "push off" action from the left hind leg that leads to better impulsion.
- The extra weight is still on the left front leg/shoulder.

Let's look at a right-handed horse hollowing and over-bending to the left:

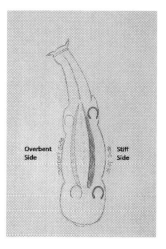

- The horse has a more flexible muscle on the left side of the spine and tighter muscle on the right side of the spine.
- This causes the left hind-leg to have a longer stride length (swinging leg) but can land slightly adducted (across).
- This transfers the horse's weight onto the diagonally opposite front leg (right front leg).
- The horse is often thought to 'drop the right shoulder in or out' and drifts to the right.

Right handed horse going to the right

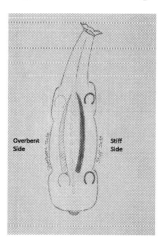

- The same right-handed horse moving to the right would find it harder to bend to the right due to the tighter back muscle on the right side of the spine.
- The right hind leg however is the straighter stepping leg even though it is generally stiffer and may step shorter. The horse is able to produce a greater "push off" action in the right hind leg.

Rider interference

It is important to recognise that riders are left or right handed also and that this leads to stiffness that the horse has to compensate for. We see this very clearly when the rider and horse are both 'left or right handed'; it is more difficult to correct the horse when the rider and horse are stiff on the same side.

Common rider position issues:

- A rider who is tight in the adductor (groin) and hip flexor muscles will block the horse's bend
- A rider who collapses in the ribcage when trying to straighten the horse will end up blocking the horse more
- The horse will often shift the rider's seat to compensate for its own crookedness.
- The rider who is too tight in the thighs and/or too tight with the reins will encourage the horse to lean
- If the rider's seat is uneven the horse has to compensate for this unbalanced position
- If the rider's reins and/or thighs are too tight while asking the horse to go forward the horse will get conflicting messages of 'stop' and 'go'.

For the horse to stay soft throughout transitions and even in lateral movements, developing horizontal and vertical balance is crucial.

Balance starts with the rider, therefore we can only expect the horse to be as balanced as the rider. The rider must be able to ride with an independent seat and be able to maintain this seat in walk, trot and canter without stirrups and reins. This is a prerequisite if we expect the horse to develop relaxation, balance, rhythm, suppleness, impulsion, straightness and ultimately collection.

There is an old saying that "a horse is only as good as the jockey who rides it". Balance is where it all starts!"

To correctly educate a horse, riders need to be realistic about their own ability. Once balance and relaxation are established, then flexibility and body straightness can be achieved.

We have to work on ourselves and acknowledge the horse's response as a reflection of our skill rather than having high expectations of what our horses should or should not be doing.

Exercises to improve balance:

A good exercise for the rider to develop their seat is to be lunged on a regular basis without stirrups and reins.

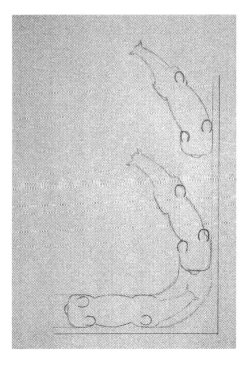

A good exercise to help improve the balance in a young horse or an older horse needing re-training is by riding shoulder-fore or shoulder-in, depending of the horse's stage of training. This is a fantastic way to be able to encourage the horse to take weight of the heavier front leg and strengthen the weaker (swinging) hind leg.

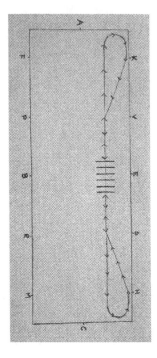

Another good exercise is to set out a series of trot poles about 5m from the track on the long side of the arena. The poles should be placed 4'-5' apart and you can start with two poles and add more poles as the horse becomes more confident until you have a total of six trot poles.

After the horse trots over the trot poles the rider stays straight for about 20m, then turns in a half 5m circle towards the arena fence and comes straight back towards the line of the trot poles. This exercise is repeated on the other side where the rider turns again in a half 5m circle towards the arena fence and comes straight back towards the line of the trot poles. This way the rider uses left and right turns evenly.

Trotting over the trot poles will help to improve the horse's horizontal balance, turning left and right on a half 5 m circle followed by a change of rein will improve the vertical balance.

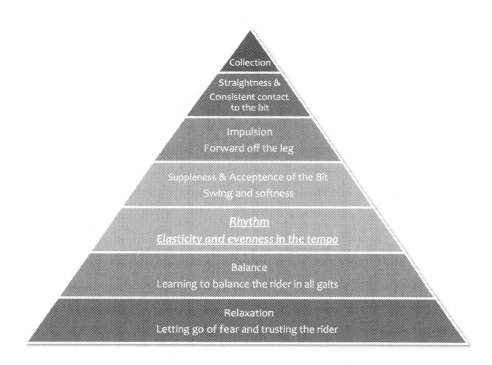

STEP 3: RHYTHM

ELASTICITY AND EVENNESS IN TEMPO

Rhythm comes from relaxation and balance. A horse that is relaxed in the environment it is schooled in and has learned to maintain horizontal and vertical balance in all three gaits will find it easier to develop rhythm.

Rhythm is the horse's ability to maintain an even gait and an even length of stride without relying on the rider. It is important that the rider has learned to stay balanced, without interfering with the horse, so the horse can initially find the tempo it is comfortable in as it develops physical strength.

Young horses training at this level should be ridden mainly in a rising trot with only short periods of sitting trot, as they are often not strong enough to carry the rider's weight over longer periods. The same goes for underdeveloped older horses in re-training. This will help to make the transition easier to the next step in the training scale "suppleness and acceptance of the bit".

Think of 'forward' as freedom of movement and un-interfered rhythm rather than speed. It is far more important for a horse to move freely and loosely than moving forward with speed.

A relaxed forward moving horse is a confident horse.

As riders, we learn that it is better for a horse to travel forward while it is establishing rhythm. I do agree with that, however I think we should re-think what is "good" forward and what is "chasing" the horse. Forward is often misinterpreted as speed.

Here are some aspects I want you to consider:

- To develop a horse's rhythm, it is very important that we consider how balanced the rider is. If the rider still struggles to maintain their balance, it will make it nearly impossible for the horse to develop rhythm.
- If an unbalanced rider blocks the horse's forwardness by being tight in the groin or by relying on the rein to 'hold onto the horse' the horse must compensate by slowing down or hollowing and rushing. Neither helps in developing rhythm.
- If an unbalanced rider is asked to ride too much forward, we end up with a 'more' unbalanced rider and an unbalanced, resisting, 'running' horse as a result.

- Many riders have embraced the concept of forwardness to develop rhythm, which is a good thing, however if we override and unbalance the horse we will disrupt the rhythm.
- If the horse is not relaxed we just end up with a rushing, tense horse. This will not develop rhythm but rather develop more tension. Remember that horses are flight animals; when a horse is under stress the flight instinct is triggered which causes the horse to run.

If the rider is unbalanced the horse cannot develop rhythm.

Tension and running

As trainers and coaches, we should re-think 'forward' when it comes to developing rhythm and instead focus on 'even, balanced movements'.

- It is therefore important that the rider assesses the horse's relaxation and balance at the beginning of each training session and adjusts the horse's tempo accordingly. A horse can still go forward in rhythm while maintaining a slower tempo.
- It is important to understand that each horse has its own rhythm and tempo at each stage of its training. If we ignore this and chase the horse, we compromise relaxation and balance and this will set the horse's training back considerably.
- For a rider to undertake training of a young horse, the rider should already have a balanced, independent seat. This will allow the rider to go with the horse without interfering, while the horse can find its own rhythm.

So many riders think of going forward as a 'getting out of trouble' tool. For example, when horses are fresh or spooky. To me choosing forwardness when trying to deal with tension is just creating more anxiety and resistance. My preference is always to create relaxation when the horse becomes tense. Therefore, relaxation is a foundation and must be established before we start training horses.

When a horse is playing up, spooky or just fresh, the rider needs to make sure all forward aids are clear and not contradicted by an unconscious blocking aid. For example, when the rider applies their lower leg the thigh and hands must stay soft so that the horse can go forward instead of the rider blocking and kicking at the same time. This requires the rider to stay relaxed as well.

When the horse is tense, forwardness alone will seldom bring the horse back to relaxation. The rider must make it a priority for the horse to start breathing out again and the best way to do this is to breathe out themselves.

TRAINING FOCUS

It is important to understand that the environment we school our horses in is very important and can either help or hinder in the horse's development of rhythm.

In Europe, most young horses are started in a stud by professional riders riding in a 20m x 40m indoor arena. Occasionally will you find a stud with a 20m x 60m indoor arena; generally, this size is for competition stables or outdoor arenas. When a young horse is schooled in a small indoor arena the horse travels only a short distance (40m) in a straight line before turning a corner, then an even shorter distance (20m) before turning another corner and so on...!

Also, what we should consider is that most professional riders in Europe actually ride a corner as a corner rather than a ¼ of a 20m circle.

The point I am making here is that a horse learns to maintain rhythm by improving their horizontal balance (forwards /backwards) and vertical balance (side to side) by travelling short distances in a straight line before rebalancing themselves automatically as they approach the corner with a solid wall behind it. The horses are ridden through the corner, which engages the hindquarters and rebalances the horse, followed by another corner where the horse rebalances as it is ridden through the corner, followed by another short distance and so on....!

This environment is very different from what we have in Australia, which is mainly an open paddock or a 20m x 60m outdoor arena with no fence. Here the horse is not automatically encouraged to find its own balance but rather learns to run and drift.

Exercises to improve rhythm:

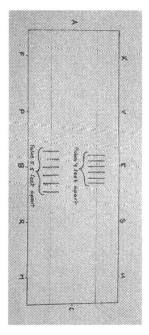

Placing a series of 5 or 6 trot poles on the track in the middle of both long sides. One set of trot poles has a distance of 4' between the poles while the other set has a distance of 5 1/2'. This allows the rider to encourage the horse to lengthen and shorten their stride and maintain an even rhythm with different tempos. The rider is encouraged to soften both reins over the poles and let the poles shorten or lengthen the stride, which encourages the horses to start thinking for themselves.

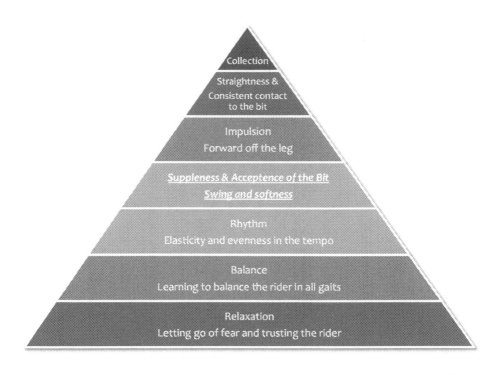

STEP 4: SUPPLENESS AND ACCEPTANCE OF THE BIT

SWING AND SOFTNESS

Suppleness develops from relaxation, balance and rhythm, which show that the horse is becoming stronger and softer through the body. Suppleness is also the alignment of the horse's spine from the poll to the tail, developing the horse's back muscles more evenly and encouraging the horse to accept the bit.

The parts of the horse's body that need to strengthen are the abdominal and back muscles. Strengthening these areas are crucial as it allows the

TANJA MITTON

horse to carry the riders weight and become more adjustable throughout the body. This will lead to the horse being able to lengthen and shorten their frame (lifting the back) and bend left and right.

As the horse's abdominal muscles become stronger it can start to soften through the back to let the rider sit, as long as the rider can sit without interfering with the horse's movements.

The expression 'letting the rider sit' means that the horse is able to maintain free movement of the back without becoming tense or resisting the rider's weight. Suppleness is all about free swinging movement, which requires a rider's position to be balanced and able to go with rather than restricting the horse's movement, especially in sitting trot and canter.

In this phase of the training process the rider still needs to address the horse's natural crookedness by improving the balance and gradually working towards straightness.

ACCEPTANCE OF THE BIT

Let me start by stating that 'acceptance of the bit' is not 'making the horse go on the bit'!

It is important at this stage that the rider makes sure that while the horse's body becomes more supple, the neck must stay long and the gullet open without the horse hollowing or resisting; this will lead to the horse being able to learn to travel freely and accept the bit.

Acceptance of the bit means that the horse maintains softness throughout the body while searching for the bit, taking the bit forward and stretching into the rein without leaning on the rider's hand. The horse needs to follow the rider's hand by lengthening and shortening the neck without becoming tense.

For a horse to stretch, the horse's hind legs need to step under. This is where the horse's abdominal muscles become engaged and the horse's back lifts up. This allows the horse to stretch into the rider's hand and look for a soft connection to the bit.

At the end of a session German trainers would say to the rider: "Zügel aus der hand kauen lassen". The direct translation means, "allowing the horse to chew the reins out of the rider's hands". When this happens we know that the horse has accepted the bit rather than holding onto, or resisting the bit.

The ideal stretch is achieved when the horse's nose stays slightly in front of the vertical line and we can draw a line from the horse's eye to the horse's hip.

If the horse's head is lower, the rider runs the risk of the horse being on the forehand.

Acceptance of the bit comes <u>because of</u> suppleness and not as a means of achieving suppleness!

Shortening the rein too much and holding a tight contact will soon lead to tension, hollowing and resistance in the horse. It will never achieve suppleness nor acceptance of the bit.

Horse is resisting the contact   Riders inside rein too tight

Some points to consider:

- First the horse must be relaxed and balanced before it can achieve suppleness and acceptance of the bit.
- For the horse to be soft and supple the rider has to be soft and supple. It is important that the horse trusts the rider's seat before it can relax and soften through the back.
- The acceptance of the bit comes from the horse's ability to lift the back whilst carrying the rider and feeling confident to stretch into the bit without being restricted by the bit.
- The horse stretching is a sign that the horse is using the muscles alongside the spine and maintaining some abdominal engagement, which makes it more comfortable to carry the rider's weight whilst staying relaxed and balanced.
- The horse's back muscles have to be developed correctly for the horse to 'let the rider sit' whilst maintaining suppleness and a swinging back throughout the ride.

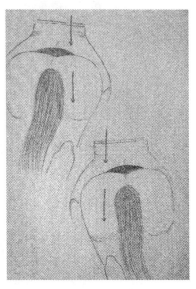

Suppleness and acceptance of the bit will help the horse to establish swing, softness and bend. To achieve this, the rider's hip movement must be in harmony with the horse's hip movement.

It is important that the rider doesn't block the horse's back but rather follows the horse's back. This is achieved by the rider maintaining softness in their hips, which allows the horse to move freely underneath the rider's seat (see Rider's Training Scale).

To form a clear connection between horse and rider, it is important the horse not only accepts the rider's seat but also, more importantly, follows the rider's seat.

Exercises to establish suppleness and acceptance of the bit:

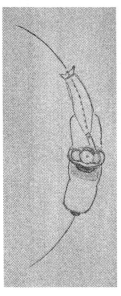

A good indication of suppleness is when the rider is able to take both reins in one hand and is still able to ride circles, straight lines, turns and transitions. This is a sign that the horse has learned to follow the rider's seat rather than the reins.

- Use drums or jumping wings as obstacles to ride turns and changes of rein. Riding these turns and changes of rein with either a loser rein or even with only one hand on the rein (no neck reining!) is a good exercise to teach the horse to follow the rider's seat.

This is the time in the horses training where we start riding lateral movements.

- Beginning with leg yielding, this can be done with the horse's head pointing towards the arena fence to help the horse to balance without 'running' towards the middle of the arena. Followed by leg yielding where the horse's head points to the inside of the arena. Then we can work on leg yielding from the track to the ¾ line.
- Shoulder-in is another good suppling exercise as well as travers. In both movements the horse learns to bend the shoulders and hindquarters independently.

Riding transitions.

- At this stage the transitions should start with halt-walk, walk-trot, trot-canter and canter-trot, trot-walk, walk-halt. At this stage the horse hasn't developed impulsion and therefore may not be ready to do a halt-trot or walk-canter transition. The canter-walk and trot-halt transitions shouldn't be practised too much either. The horse that has not developed impulsion is more inclined to 'fall' into the transition and becomes heavy on the forehand by blocking the shoulders.

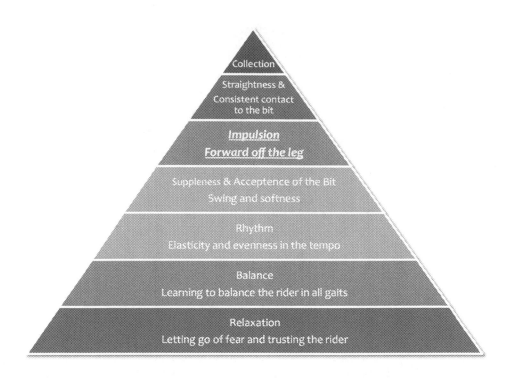

The pyramid from bottom to top:

Relaxation
Letting go of fear and trusting the rider

Balance
Learning to balance the rider in all gaits

Rhythm
Elasticity and evenness in the tempo

Suppleness & Acceptence of the Bit
Swing and softness

Impulsion
Forward off the leg

Straightness &
Consistent contact
to the bit

Collection

STEP 5: IMPULSION

FORWARD OFF THE LEG

After the first 4 steps of the pyramid are in place and the rider can sit in the correct position, the horse's hind legs are activated and the horse is encouraged to lift even more through the back. By stepping the hind legs forward and under its body and swinging its back freely, the horse develops more strength and allows the rider to sit. The rider must make sure that they sit evenly, allowing the horse's back to lift so that the rider does not block the horse's forward movement (explained in the Rider's Training Scale step 3 to 5).

The horse has to learn to take more weight on the hind legs by tilting the pelvis and lifting the back. This will activate and strengthen the hocks allowing the horse to 'push' more from behind and develop impulsion.

IMPULSION

- For the horse to develop impulsion, the rider must engage their core and rotate their pelvis by lifting the pubic bone to make room for the horse's back to lift.
- To increase strength in the hind legs the horse also has to rotate their pelvis and engage their core.
- Just like the rider, the horse does not have a naturally strong core. Muscles need to be exercised and strengthened to be able to maintain long-term engagement, develop more impulsion and encourage self-carriage. A horse with a weak core will develop a hollow back and will most likely experience discomfort when ridden over long periods. This naturally will lead to tension and resistance due to incorrect muscle development and pain.
- The horse must maintain an acceptance of the bit while going forward. Staying soft in the jaw (chewing and licking) allows the poll to stay relaxed.

LAZY HORSE, HOT HORSE

When riding a horse forward from the leg, it is important that the rider doesn't block the forwardness. A rider who is stiff in the hips and therefore tips onto the pubic bone automatically creates tightness in their groin and thighs. This acts like a hand-break, which blocks the horse from moving forward and lifting their back. If the horse is then asked to go forward it will either resist the forwardness, tense up, or rush, as they have to 'squeeze' through the blockage.

The horse will seem like it is either not responding to the rider's legs or overreacting to the rider's legs depending on the horse's personality, state of mind and physical development.

It is therefore very important for the rider to learn to sit correctly to develop true forwardness from the leg (explained in the Rider's Training Scale).

When the horse moves forward from the leg it needs to maintain relaxation, balance and softness through the back and poll while engaging the hind legs (rotating the pelvis and engaging the core). This way the rider increases impulsion rather than encourages the horse to run.

Exercises to improve Impulsion:

- Riding transitions (halt – trot, walk – canter)
- Riding transitions within the pace (lengthening and shortening strides)
- Lengthening and shortening the stride over poles; The pole evenly placed on the circle (see diagram) is a great way to establish

rhythm and stride length while maintaining relaxation/balance. With the distances described, a line over the middle of the poles should be a comfortable, balanced 3 canter strides for most horses. Once balance and relaxation has been established, try riding an inside line in a shorter, more balanced canter to practice your half halt. Then ride an outside line in either 4 regular strides or 3 longer strides to engage the hind legs and establish impulsion. The ultimate exercise would be to ride one circle on the middle line in a working canter, half-halt, move to the inside track in a collecting canter then lengthen the stride while moving to the outside track.

This exercise can also be ridden in the trot with the same aims of establishing rhythm and balance to then move on to improving impulsion and length of stride.

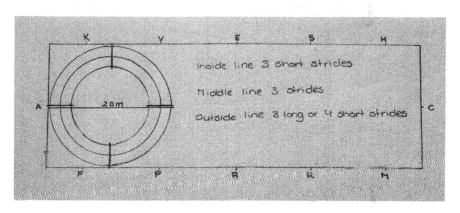

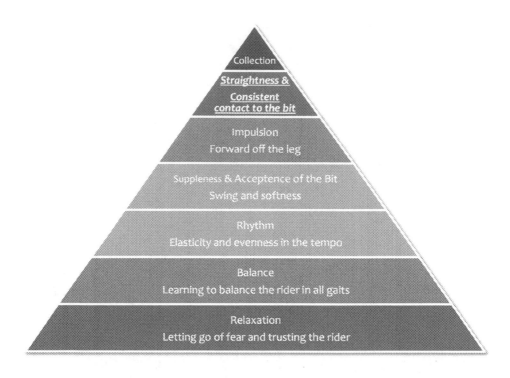

The pyramid, from top to bottom:

Collection

Straightness & Consistent contact to the bit

Impulsion
Forward off the leg

Suppleness & Acceptance of the Bit
Swing and softness

Rhythm
Elasticity and evenness in the tempo

Balance
Learning to balance the rider in all gaits

Relaxation
Letting go of fear and trusting the rider

STEP 6: STRAIGHTNESS & CONSISTENT CONTACT TO THE BIT

The muscles along the horse's back need to be evenly developed without one side being tighter than the other. The horse should be able to step through straight with both hind legs without adducting (stepping inwards underneath their body) or abducting (stepping outwards and blocking the ribcage) to produce the same 'push off power' that travels through the horse's body. The horse must learn to take weight onto both hind legs and in particular, keep the weight on the inside hind leg in a turn or circle without transferring the weight onto the opposite shoulder. Only then does the horse have true straightness.

Crookedness comes from the horse carrying uneven weight in their front-legs (dropping the shoulder in or out) and adducting or abducting the back legs (swinging quarters in or out).

It is now expected that the horse has reached a stage in the training process where it has developed its horizontal and vertical balance with enough strength in their body to allow the weight to be carried evenly in all four legs while being able to shift weight into their hind legs, allowing the front legs to be lighter.

The horse is then able to fully develop straightness.

Exercises to straighten the swinging hind leg:

The rider should be able to identify the horse's crookedness (right or left-handed) and shift the uneven weight from the horse's front-legs into their back-legs. The horse then has to learn to carry even weight in both back legs by changing the way it travels. Instead of adducting one or both back-legs (stepping across) the horse must learn to step forward with straightness. This will allow the horse to keep the hind-legs in line with the front-legs and therefore carry even weight into a turn and on the straight line.

A good way to straighten and strengthen the weaker 'swinging' hind leg is to ride a shoulder-in with the leg that needs correcting on the outside.

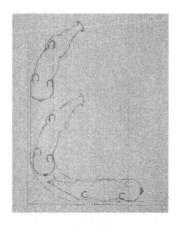

Also walk, trot and canter pirouettes are all exercises that help in developing even weight bearing in both hind legs that in turn develops straightness.

With the young horse we start in the walk with turns on the haunches and increasing and decreasing the circle in the walk and trot. The importance is to have a supple horse that is able to shift their weight from one shoulder into the opposite hind leg in both directions. Correct flexion and counter flexion is required to instigate the shift. However, it is important for the rider to understand that it is not only about the flexion of the horse but more so the correct seat of the rider.

Straightness is achieved:

- When a horse can maintain relaxation, balance and suppleness.
- Has developed strength in the back legs by being able to maintain core engagement and pelvis rotation.
- Can move straight in all three paces rather than moving crooked, which is generally compensating for training faults, either in the rider's seat or the horse's development. (Refer to step 2 – Balance in the Rider Training Scale).
- Has the ability to maintain weight in the inside hind leg at all times, especially in turns and circles. (Pirouette)
- Horses tend to adduct particularly in a turn and on the circle and this is where true straightness will show up.

CONSISTENT CONTACT

A consistent contact is important to achieve frame and outline in a horse. The contact sets boundaries and encourages the horse to stay in a frame while maintaining softness throughout the poll and body.

It is important to make sure that the contact is not used to 'make' the horse straight but rather to maintain alignment from the horse's poll through to the horse's body without restricting the horse's movement or the elasticity in the swing. The rider has to remember to have 'forward thinking hands' and allow the horse to move forward into the bit.

The contact can never be a 'pulling back' contact or a 'jamming up' contact. The horse should be able to maintain the same movement and rhythm with or without a contact and that the horse's frame maintains an open gullet with the horse's nose staying slightly in front of the vertical.

It is important to understand that contact is achieved by the rider riding the horse forward into the bit rather than 'pulling' backwards.

We often see horses being forced into a false frame that they are not able to sustain. This generally happens due to weaknesses and a misunderstanding or shortcut in the early steps of the training scale.

It is very important that all the previous steps are established and that a consistent contact is maintained before we continue the training process towards collection.

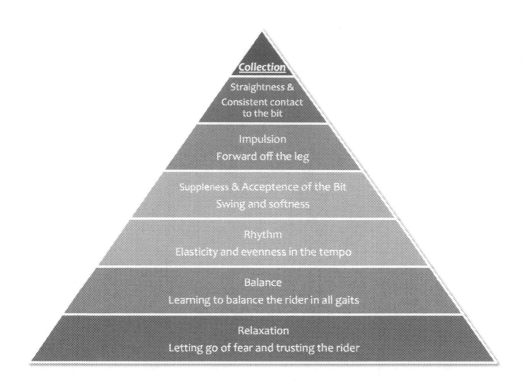

STEP 7: COLLECTION

ENGAGEMENT, LIGHTNESS AND SELF-CARRIAGE

Collection refers to the horse's posture. It is achieved by the horse's ability to lengthen and shorten their body while maintaining core engagement, a supple back, an open gullet and a head carriage where the poll is the highest point with the horse's nose staying on or in front of the vertical.

The horse must be able to maintain core engagement, which leads to the horse's back being well developed and strong enough to support and instigate the lengthening and shortening by lifting and relaxing the back. The horse's hocks take on a higher degree of bend as they carry more of the horse's weight.

As the horses' movements become more collected, the strides become shorter without losing swing or impulsion and this leads to more cadence. (Piaffe and Passage)

The horse becomes lighter in the contact as it becomes lighter in the front legs and the back legs carry more weight; the horse develops self-carriage.

This means that the horse's neck lifts and the poll becomes the highest point as the hindquarters lower and take on more weight. The neck shortens as the horse's body shortens, but it is important to note that the gullet must stay open and the nose must stay on the vertical not dropping behind.

The ultimate movements in collection are passage, piaffe and levade, which not only require the horse to shorten the body and lift the back, but also maintain strength and engagement in the hind legs to carry the majority of the horse's weight, which in turn creates lightness and cadence.

Collection is the horse's ability to maintain self-carriage due to balance and a consistency in contact (explained in the Rider's Training Scale step 6).

This creates an 'uphill' impression, which can only be achieved when the horse is ridden by a balanced rider, 'from behind into the bit'.

If the horse's head and neck are forced to lift without the correct training to develop the necessary strength, the result will be that the horse hollows through the back and disengages the hind legs.

This will cause lots of problems!

A well-trained horse will be able to maintain the correct position for longer periods.

SUMMARY

Looking at the previous two training scales, it becomes obvious that just like in any other team sport, each member must be at their best to achieve team success.

First the rider must learn to go with the horse by developing balance and an independent seat so that they don't hinder the natural movement of the horse.

Then the rider must learn to positively influence the horse's movement without interfering with it.

Lastly the rider becomes a trainer when they can develop the horse's movement by guiding it through the steps of the training scale.

A rider needs lots of experience and 'feel' to go from being a 'rider' to becoming a 'trainer'. This step is like the graduation from college, it is not a given, it has to be earned.

If the process is rushed it creates problems. Inexperienced riders taking shortcuts due to lack of skill and understanding often cause these problems.

The rider needs to have a sound understanding of the foundational training of horses as well as being physically capable. Only a horse and rider who are physically and mentally fit are able to perform at their best.

This is why I would always encourage riders to have themselves checked and treated by a Chiropractor, Physiotherapist or other health professional at the same time as they have their horses treated. There is no point in having one member of the team straightened out while the other is still crooked.

The Mindset Training Scale

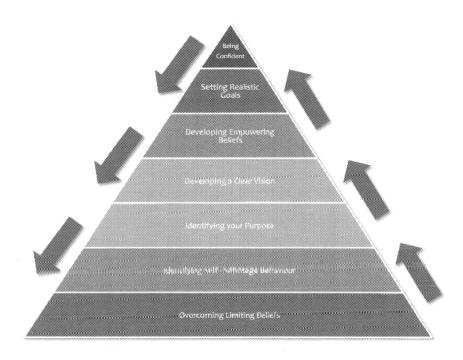

> **"PERSONAL CHANGE COMES ABOUT WHEN WE BECOME**
> **COMFORTABLE WITH BEING UNCOMFORTABLE."**
> **- TANJA MITTON**

The rider's mindset is the area that is most forgotten or misunderstood in our equestrian industry. No matter what discipline, we rarely address the way a rider thinks.

The reason I have put together a rider's mindset training scale is because this is an integral part of success in training the rider and the horse. Our own state of mind reflects on how we deal with situations as they come up and how we react to people and horses around us.

Everything we do is generally a reflection of how we feel about ourselves. If we are happy and content, achieving our goals and living our purpose we are much more comfortable with ourselves and compassionate to others.

On the contrary, if we are unhappy and irritated, failing in our achievements and living someone else's life, we are more inclined to judge others around us.

Horses are the best personal development coaches we can work with because of their consistent, honest and non-judgemental feedback.

To become the best rider we can be we have to become the best person we can be first. Leadership is not about domination and strength but rather cooperation and understanding.

Successful riders and coaches have to be successful people first.

I believe that success cannot be measured by how many trophies we win, but more so by how many lives we effect. We affect the lives of horses and people by sharing love and compassion.

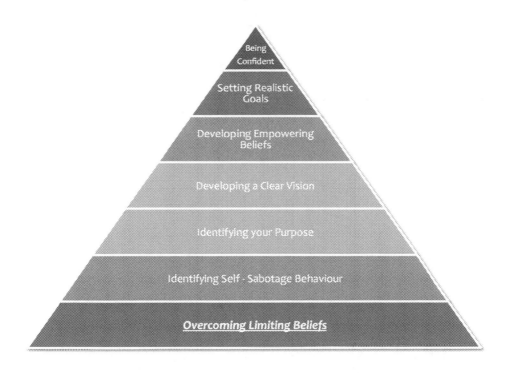

STEP 1: OVERCOMING LIMITING BELIEFS

Limiting beliefs often start when we are very young and are shaped by what other people say to us and the experiences we have while growing up. Our environment and the people around us play a huge role in how we see ourselves and the beliefs we take on. Limiting beliefs are often pure illusion and have no relevance to reality, however by identifying with them and putting focus to them we make them part of our reality. Most people end up living their entire life holding onto their limiting beliefs and taking action according to what they believe they can or they can't do.

Common limiting beliefs are:

- I am not good enough
    I. To succeed at a certain level
    II. To make a team selection
    III. To be someone special

- I am not worthy
    I. To be noticed
    II. To associate with riders that are better than me
    III. To have a good horse and own nice gear

- Lack of finance
    I. I'll never be successful because I can't afford an expensive horse
    II. You need money to be a successful professional rider
    III. Even when I work hard I only just have enough money

- Always unlucky
    I. I am always the unlucky one
    II. No matter how hard I try good things never happen to me
    III. Whenever things are going well it is only a matter of time before everything falls apart again

We all have an image of ourselves that details who we are and what we can or can't do, our talents and abilities, our faults and limitations. These images become the road map of our actions. They determine our behaviour, what we say and how we react to our day-to-day experiences. Most people find it easier to see qualities in others rather than in themselves and therefore we tend to encourage other people around us much more then we encourage ourselves.

Start by writing out a list of your limiting beliefs. What negative beliefs have you taken on in your lifetime and where did they come from?

Think about what people have said to you in the past:

- Parents
- Friends
- Riding instructors
- Judges

Write out how this has affected you and how your beliefs changed your view on life and your resultant behaviour.

A desire to change by becoming consciously aware of your limiting beliefs is the first step to making changes.

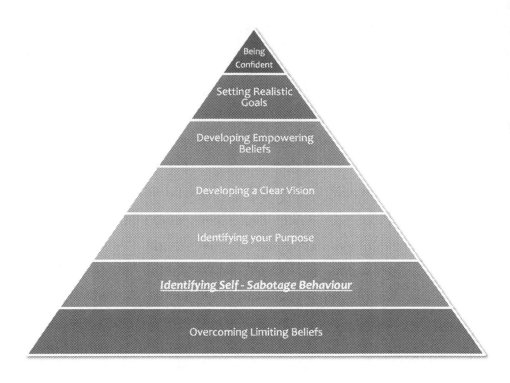

Step 2: Identifying Self-Sabotage Behaviour

The behaviour that comes from limiting beliefs is what we call self-sabotage.

Think of it this way; like most human beings, we generally like to be right. That means that when we have decided that for example 'we are not good enough' we look for proof that our belief is correct.

For example, typical self- sabotage behaviour is:

- A rider who believes that they are not good enough to ride successfully at elementary level dressage may rush to the first elementary competition too soon. Without enough preparation, on a competition ground that they and their horse have had a bad experience at previously they could very easily set themselves up for failure before they even begin.

- A rider who believes that they are not worthy to be noticed by riders who are 'better' than they are might be at a big competition looking to strike up conversations with riders who they admire, just as they are getting ready to get on their horse and compete. Due to 'bad timing' the rider might be cutting that person short or seem to be abrupt, which again confirms the belief 'they don't want to have anything to do with me'.

- Riders with a belief that they don't have enough money might sabotage themselves when they look to buy a new horse. Instead of looking at horses that fit into their price range, they might look at horses that are far too expensive just to confirm that they can't find the right horse and they have a lack of finance.

- A rider who feels that they are always unlucky might be more inclined to buy a horse that has some previous history of injuries, unsoundness or physical/mental problems and is therefore at a higher risk of something going wrong.

Limiting beliefs are very powerful and have a big impact on our actions, which determine the outcomes we get.

Our language and self-talk also has a huge influence on our behaviour and clearly reflects our limiting beliefs.

Words like:

- I'll try
- I'll see how I go
- It's probably not going to happen
- I wish
- I won't get my hopes up

These are all non-committal words and reflect uncertainty and a lack of real belief.

To overcome these, make a list of your behavioural patterns and start to look for potential self-sabotage strategies.

Again self-awareness is the first step to making changes.

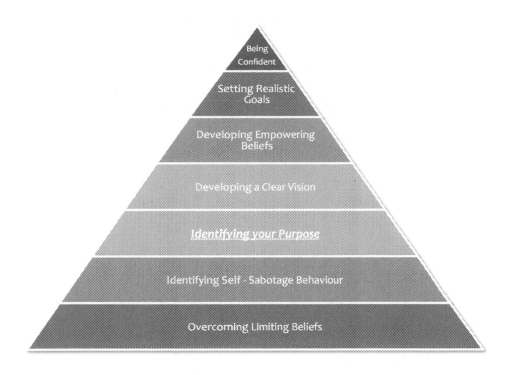

Step 3: Identifying Your Purpose

I believe a lot of riders struggle because they haven't identified their purpose.

Purpose is knowing why you are doing what you are doing.

Your purpose is your WHY; it gives you the drive to keep going and keeps the fire going within you.

Your purpose also helps you to stay on track and follow your path rather than getting side tracked onto someone else's path.

This can be explained easier in the following examples:

- If you are passionate about educating horses and taking your time with each individual horse you might come across people who want to take you down the path of competition or climbing the competition ladder too quickly. This can become a conflict within you over time.

If your purpose is to educate and train horses, competition and getting from one level to the next might not be your main priority. Therefore it is important to know your purpose and follow it.

- If your purpose is to compete and be the best you can be, being in an environment of riders who want to ride for fun might not be the appropriate place because it is not aligned with *your* purpose.

Here are some examples outside of riding:

- If your purpose is to help and encourage people and you are placed in a role at work where you have to collect debt then that can again cause inner conflict.
- If your purpose is financial independence and you enjoy making money you don't want to be around people who see money as a negative because they have a limiting belief around it.

In the above examples it is important to note that there is no right or wrong way, it is simply different purposes that drive different actions and produce different outcomes.

Knowing your purpose will also help you stay on track and keep your enthusiasm. It also helps when you talk to other people about what fires you up. This is particularly important for professional riders when they talk to their sponsors and owners as well as for coaches communicating with their students.

Spend some time writing down your purpose, WHY you do what you do and this will help develop your vision for the future.

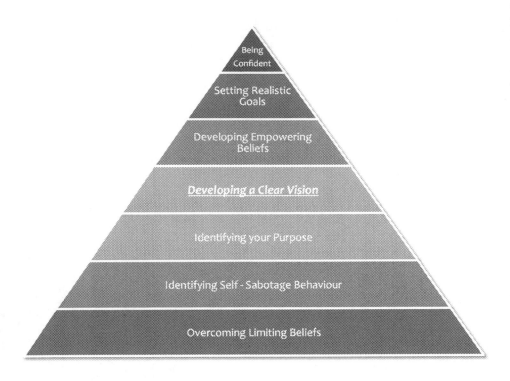

Step 4: Develop a Clear Vision

Now that you have found your purpose, it is time to start to develop your vision for the future. Your vision is different from your goals. Vision is the big picture of your ideal life. Creating an idea of who you can become and what you can achieve when you align with your purpose.

When you develop a clear vision of your future, make sure you dream big!

Allow yourself to step out of your comfort zone. It is ok to create a picture of yourself that is bigger than your current self and stretches your comfort zone.

Remember what you tell your friends. You encourage them by saying things like:

- You can do that
- You are just as good as other people are and if you are prepared to do the work and you give it time you'll get there
- Anything is possible
- Look how far you have come already. Did you think you would achieve what you have done when you first started out?

In order to believe in your vision, you have to know what your purpose is, become your own best friend and start to encourage yourself rather than put yourself down. This is a vital step forward.

Your vision creates your road map; a path that you can follow. Occasionally you will come across some detours or even roadblocks. If you go on holidays and travel from A to B, you don't cancel your holiday and go back home just because of road works and a couple of detours. No, you change plans if you need to, take more time and leave the path you were on short term until you find a way around whatever is blocking your holiday destination. Take the same approach to your life and the vision you have of yourself.

A vision board is a great way to help you develop this clear vision and turn it into pictures that can serve as a constant reminder of where you want to go and who you want to be. Remember, a picture paints a 1000 words.

Vision Board

HOW TO CREATE A VISION BOARD

A vision board is a great way to capture your vision in pictures. You can get really creative when it comes to making a vision board and there is no limit to your imagination.

First decide what the vision board is all about. It can be to help you make changes to your position, creating a clear vision of your dreams or providing you with an image of what the end result will look like. By making it as real as possible it is easy to see yourself already achieving it before you even start.

Start by getting a big colorful piece of cardboard like the ones kids use for projects.

TANJA MITTON

Let's say you are creating a vision board to help with some positional changes. Get some old horse magazines and find pictures that show the position you are aiming for.

Then take the pictures, cut them out and place them on your vision board. To make them more effective you can replace the riders' head with your own. The more real you can make it the better it is. The idea is that you can look at the picture and you can see, feel and imagine yourself in it.

It is much easier to achieve changes that you can see. Know what you are looking for, be really clear on it and it will be much more achievable.

Have fun creating your vision board!

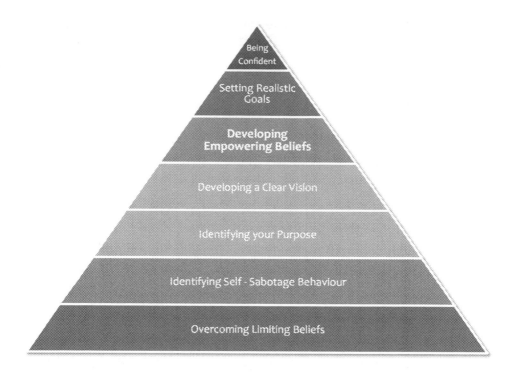

STEP 5: DEVELOP EMPOWERING BELIEFS

The opposite of limiting beliefs are empowering beliefs. Empowering beliefs are the beliefs you want to hold onto. They reinforce all the things you are good at, everything you can do and all the things you are achieving.

Trust in yourself is vital step to develop empowering beliefs. Understand that there will always be people who agree with what you say and do, and people who don't agree with you, and that is ok. The important part is not to have everyone agreeing with you but rather being able to stand up for what you believe in.

Tanja Mitton

There is seldom a clear right and wrong but rather an opinion and different ways on how to do things. If you try to please everyone you run the risk of pleasing no one, particularly yourself.

The most important thing is to trust your own judgment and to understand that what is right for you today may not be right for you tomorrow. This does not make it right one day and wrong the next; it rather reflects growth and learning. You grow with every experience and change because of them.

I often speak to riders who are overwhelmed by how much there is to learn and sometimes the advice can be overwhelming, leaving a rider feeling very inadequate and insecure.

My advice to these riders is:

- When asking for advice choose wisely who you ask
- Free advice is often worth nothing
- The more knowledgeable someone is the less they force advice onto others
- There is seldom a right or wrong but rather a different way of how to do things

Developing empowering beliefs takes time and experience. There is a lifetime worth of learning out there so don't be in a rush to discover everything in a couple of years.

The more you know the more you realise you don't know!

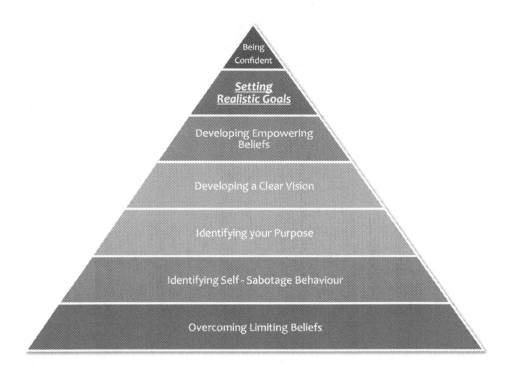

STEP 6: SET REALISTIC GOALS

When it comes to goal setting there is a whole book that can be written on just this topic alone.

Most riders make the mistake that they set goals that are driven by their limiting beliefs and therefore the goals are part of their self-sabotage strategies, setting themselves up for failure rather than success.

There is a very well known and proven formula for goal setting, called the SMART Goals process.

SMART Goals stands for:

Specific

- Make the goal specific. A goal that states that you want to improve your riding is not specific enough. It needs to have a clearer definition of what the area you want to improve in is and what it looks like.

Measurable

- Make sure you can clearly measure the outcome so you know when the goal has been achieved.

Achievable

- Check the goal is achievable and within your control. Unachievable goals are often driven by self-sabotage and limiting beliefs.

Relevant

- Is the goal relevant to your purpose and your vision? Does it fit in with your other goals and plans?

Timed

- Think about the time frame in which you want to achieve your goal. Again too many riders set themselves up for failure by setting a goal with an unrealistic timeframe.

Goal setting should be fun and inspire you to achieve greater things. When you align your goals through the SMART goal checklist, break them down. Like the saying "The Great Wall of China was built one stone at the time", the same applies for your goals, especially if they are bigger, longer timeframe goals. Rather than looking at the whole, break them down into bite size chunks. A big goal can be overwhelming but as soon as you can see each single step that you need to achieve it, the whole goal becomes a lot more achievable.

Most people have set goals in some area of their life either for work, school, holidays or an ultimate goal such as organising a wedding. The process is the same.

How many people do you know that have cancelled their wedding the week before just because they didn't get organised in time??

It is time to commit to your goals and start actively working on them. Make a commitment to yourself and get going.

Remember to enjoy the journey.

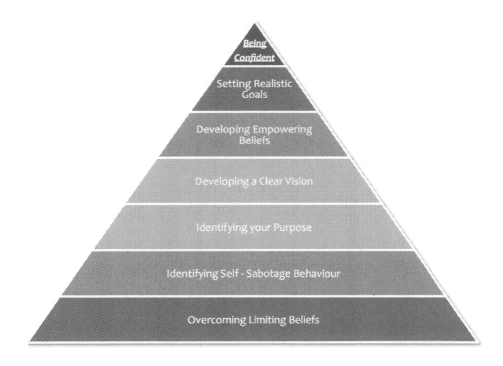

Step 7: Being Confident

Confidence is at the top of the mindset training scale because it is the outcome of all the steps combined rather than the first step.

We have to address the following steps:

1. Overcoming our limiting beliefs so that we are not defined by our past but can move forward into the future

2. Identifying self-sabotage patterns so that we become aware of our behaviour and are able to make better choices.

3. Identifying our purpose keeps us motivated and helps us to stay committed when change becomes uncomfortable.

4. Developing a clear vision helps to create a new image of ourselves that we can start modelling our behaviour and action on.

5. With experience and time comes an empowering belief. This happens when we 'own our stuff'. Empowering beliefs come with a 'can do' attitude.

6. This will help us to achieve the goals we set ourselves because we are more likely to take the correct action and follow through with the process.

7. Confidence is a state of mind and the realisation that most of what we have to overcome is in our head. We buy into our emotions and see them as reality when really it's just a thought, a feeling, a 'what if' question.

Being confident does not mean we know everything there is, it rather reflects humbleness that comes from the realisation of how far we have come.

Confidence is compassion for others, horses and riders, and the wisdom to know when to give advice and when to be silent.

Confidence is respecting the horse and learning from it rather than dominating it.

Confidence is owning what you know and knowing how much more there is to learn.

Confidence is knowing when to ask for help and who to ask.

Confidence is trusting your gut instinct and learning when to listen and when to shrug it off (or a hug ☺) as you let go.

Confidence is certainty, not letting your ego get involved, or the need to be proven right. When you are confident you can walk away because you know you don't have to prove yourself by winning an argument.

I am often asked if being confident means you are prepared to get on any horse and ride whatever is asked of you. My answer is no, that is not what I see as confidence. Being confident to me is walking away from a horse that is bucking because I don't need to prove myself in front of others. I would rather find out why the horse feels a need to buck in the first place and get to the cause so I can deal with the real issue and make it better for the horse.

Confidence to me is having knowledge, understanding and the wisdom to keep learning.

SUMMARY

I hope this book has served the purpose it was designed for.

My purpose was to explain the already existing German training scale in simple words that can make sense to riders of all levels.

By developing the rider position training scale my aim is to make riders and coaches more aware of how important the rider is in the partnership. The mindset training scale is to give a guideline on how we can develop ourselves personally.

As I stated in the beginning of the book, these are my personal beliefs and views on training horses and riders. I am not a physiotherapist, dressage trainer or psychologist. I am a NLP Master Coach and Rider Position Coach. I am a rider who has had a lifetime of experience in working with horses and riders. Learning by making many mistakes and succeeding by sticking with it through the tough times. My passion for education and my love of horses and people are the drive behind this book. If you can find one thing in this book that helps you become a better rider/person then my personal efforts have been worthwhile.

Happy riding everyone ☺

Printed in the United States
By Bookmasters